GW01250312

This Book Belongs To:

....

....

....

Hello, this is me

cut picture of your child
to size and stick here

My name is ....
I am ....years/months old

Cut and stick your drawing here

Can you draw a picture of yourself?

This is where I live

cut picture of your home
to size and stick here

I share my home with my family

Can you find the baby hidden in the picture?

What colour is the front door?

How many flowers can you see?

This is my family

cut picture of your family
to size and stick here

We are having a baby!

Can you find the baby hidden in the picture?

What colour is the train?

How many cakes can you see?

Our baby is growing inside my mummy's tummy

cut picture of mummy and bump
to size and stick here

Sometimes when I sit really quiet I can feel the baby moving

Can you find the baby hidden in the picture?

What colour is the car?

How many balls can you see?

Sometimes Mummy has to go to the hospital

The doctors make sure that mummy and baby are well

Can you find the baby hidden in the picture?
What colour is the clock?
How many books can you see?

This is a picture of our baby inside my mummy's tummy on the Hospital TV

cut picture of your scan
to size and stick here

Is it a boy or is it a girl? What would you like best - a brother or a sister?

Can you find the baby hidden in the picture?
What colour is the lampshade?
How many teddies can you see?

Our baby is due in..

I can't wait to be a big brother/sister. I can share all my toys

Can you find the baby hidden in the picture?
What colour is the skipping rope?
How many pictures can you see?

Hooray! Mummy has had our baby!
Our baby's name is...................................

cut picture of your new baby
to size and stick here

I am now a big brother/sister.
I am the best big brother/sister in the world.

Can you find the baby hidden in the picture?
What colour is the biggest balloon?
How many balloons can you see?

This is my bigger family

cut picture of your bigger family
to size and stick here

I love having a BIGGER family